Wild West Adventures

Wild West Adventures

Donna Vann

CF4·K

For Charlie and Zachary, with love

Special thanks to the many people who helped with details of the Wild West then and now, including The George Ranch Historical Park in Richmond, Texas.

© Copyright 2006 Donna Vann
ISBN 978-1-84550-065-8

Published in 2006 and reprinted in 2011 by
Christian Focus Publications,
Geanies House, Fearn, Tain
Ross-shire, IV20 1TW,
Great Britain

Cover design by Daniel van Straaten
Cover illustration by Graham Kennedy
Other illustrations by Fred Apps

Scripture Version used throughout: New Living Translation.
Holy Bible, New Living Translation, copyright 1996 by Tyndale
Charitable Trust

Printed and bound by Bell and Bain, Glasgow

Contents

Welcome to the Wild West!

What was it like to trek in a bumpy covered wagon across the vast Plains, to begin a new and dangerous life with your family in the Wild West? How did it feel to be a tough cowboy, riding all day on a horse under the blazing sun or in the blinding snow, always on the lookout for Indians and deadly snakes? What were some of the strange creatures and plant life of the American West?

After the Revolutionary War in the late 1700's, America's border reached just beyond the Appalachian Mountains to the west of the original colonies. But in 1803 President Thomas Jefferson took a huge gamble - he paid 15 million dollars to buy the 'Louisiana Purchase' from France. This doubled the size of the US. By the mid-1800's America owned all the land from the Atlantic to the Pacific oceans.

People began to head west to seek their fortune. At first there were the 'Mountain Men' who mainly trapped beaver, or explorers who traveled around just to see what this vast surprising land looked like. They were followed by people seeking gold in California, or pioneer families trying to find free land to settle on. Some came all the way from Europe, eager for the chance of a fresh start in a new country. Others were slaves freed after the Civil War, who could not afford land in the South. Of course there were already people living in the West, the original Americans known as Indians.

The Wild West covered about two-thirds of what is now the continental United States. It stretched from the Mississippi River all the way to the Pacific Ocean. Although the 1800's may seem like the distant past, here's a puzzle for you: one 'generation' is the age of parents when they have their first child. Assuming that is about twenty-five years, how many generations are there between the end of the Wild West around 1900 and you, living in the present day? It may not be as long ago as you think!

Many qualities of the American people came out of the western frontier: curiosity, a desire to explore, the feeling that you can get things done and then move on to the next challenge. Would you like to be an explorer, discovering something new? You can do that as you read this book and learn more about the Wild West. You may also discover some new things about being a follower of Jesus, along the way.

When the Cowboy Was King

The cowboy slides out of his saddle and onto the hard-packed dirt. The setting sun streaks the sky with purple, but he's too tired to notice. The smell of strong coffee wafts from the bunkhouse. All he can think about is washing up and getting some grub, before he falls into his bunk for an exhausted sleep. His work will start again at first light tomorrow. He pats his sweaty horse gratefully, leading it over to the barn for a rubdown and its feed bag before taking care of himself.

The cowboy was the king of the west, because pretty much everything to do with cattle depended on him. He wore special leather boots and a hat just like cowboys wear today, but he didn't drive a truck. He went everywhere on his horse. That horse was the dearest creature in the world to him - sometimes even more than his wife or kids!

In the early days the land wasn't fenced in, so the cowboy would have to ride many a mile around the ranch, to bring back an animal that had strayed too far. Some of the ranches were enormous. The King Ranch in south Texas covered an area of land about the size of Rhode Island in the US, or twice the size of Greater London! It is still a working ranch today.

As he rode the ranch, the cowboy had to watch out for rustlers. Even after the open range began to be fenced in, thieves on horses could cut the barbed wire and ride off with a whole herd of cattle. The same thing happens today, only the rustlers load the cattle into trucks and drive quietly away.

That's why every head of cattle had to be branded with the symbol of that ranch. (A 'head' is one animal.) Of course, the calf wasn't in the mood to stand still while being stuck with a hot iron! Two cowboys known as 'flankers' would sit at opposite ends of the calf. They held its legs stretched out so the 'brander' could do his job.

The brander would stick the flat end of the metal branding iron into a fire and hold it there long enough to get really hot. Then he would press it into the calf's rump with just the right pressure and a rocking motion, to make sure the whole brand showed up. Here are some famous cattle brands:

Running W; Three Feathers ; Bible; Four Sixes; Hog Eye; Bow and Arrow; Tumbling T.

A calf was always branded just after it was weaned from its mother, if possible. Any unbranded animal over six months of age was considered a 'maverick'. In the mid-1850's in Texas, a cattleman named Samuel A. Maverick owned a large herd which he had no time to brand, so they were left to run wild. After a while ranchers began to say 'That's a Maverick' whenever they saw a head of cattle without a brand, and the name stuck.

Branding a calf may sound cruel, but an animal loose on the range without a brand is fair game to anyone who wants

to steal it. If it has a brand, rustlers have to brand over the original marks to make it look like their own. For example, a *C* could easily become an *O* or a *V* could be turned into a *W*. In the days of the Old West, a rustler could be hanged for changing a brand! The best brands are ones like the famous 'Four Sixes' brand which can't be changed into something else.

It's not only calves that are mavericks. People can be too! Today we use the word to mean anyone who is unruly and wants to go his or her own way, without bothering about what a teacher or parent says.

Sheep can also be mavericks. Maverick sheep may wander off looking for greener grass, and have even been known to leap off a cliff. If another follows, then another, pretty soon there will be a big pile of dead sheep at the bottom of the cliff!

Jesus sometimes referred to his followers as 'sheep' and he described himself as the Good Shepherd. He knows we can wander off sometimes, just doing what we want and not paying any attention to him. We can get into trouble ourselves and also lead others astray. Or maybe we're in trouble just because we've followed the wrong person, like the flock of sheep that plunged over the cliff. If we do stray, Jesus will come looking for us. If we belong to him, he has promised that he will never abandon us. If you are not sure you belong to Jesus, keep reading - I will talk about that in the next chapter.

One of the cowboy's main jobs was working the big 'roundups' every spring and fall. All the cattle were herded together for branding and to decide which ones would go to market. If a cow needed to be given a pill for de-worming, the cowboy would put the pill in his palm with some whiskey or tobacco to sweeten it - then he would stick his arm all the way down the cow's throat and drop the pill inside its stomach! Fortunately for him, cows have no gag reflex and have front teeth only on the bottom of their mouths.

In the Wild West days the type of cattle raised in Texas was called the Longhorn. The horns of the Longhorn steer could be longer from tip to tip than the height of a man. They are still bred today but are not as popular as other breeds for eating.

In the late 1800's, just after the Civil War between the northern and southern states, Texas cowboys came back home to find cattle running loose and wild all over the state. Texas had too many cattle, but back East there were hardly any. In the northern and eastern US, a head of cattle would bring up to forty dollars (about £22). That was nearly as much as a cowboy made in two months!

Texas didn't have a railroad system at the time, so they had to figure out a way to get the animals up to the railroads or markets in Kansas. As a result, the famous 'cattle drives' began. The cowboys would round up the steers that were ready for market, and herd them the 800 miles (1300 kilometers) up the Chisholm Trail or one of the other cattle trails. These were broad areas for the cattle to travel on, where they would be able to find plenty of grass and water.

Imagine being a cowboy on the drive - the scorching heat, the constant smell of cattle dung, the taste of dust in your mouth as you rode in the hard saddle day after day. The cowboy always wore a scarf or 'bandana' around his neck, so he could cover his mouth if the dust got too bad. It also kept the worst of the sun off the back of his neck. His hat was a good sun protector too, and could be used as a drinking bowl if needed!

It took about three months to drive the cattle to Kansas, at a slow pace of 10 miles (sixteen kilometers) a day. The cowboy had to look out for Indians, as well as cattle thieves. When the herd was driven too fast, they would lose weight and be too scrawny to sell. If they went at a relaxed pace and had plenty to eat and enough water, they could arrive even fatter than when they started out. Contented cattle were also less likely to charge.

Even so, cattle were easily spooked. The crack of a rifle could set them off, or a crash of thunder, or even a loud sneeze. And then - stampede! The terrified animals would bolt in panic.

After the stampede died down, the men would round up any runaway steers. A cowboy had to be able to hit the moving target of a panicky steer while his horse was galloping at full speed! He carried a long coiled rope called a 'lariat' or 'lasso'. When he was close enough the cowboy would quickly tie one end of his rope to the saddle horn and toss out the loop end to drop down over the steer's horns. His horse knew what to do - it would stop dead still so the rope would go taut.

A cowboy's gear was designed to help him in all his tasks. His leather boots would quickly slip out of the stirrup when he had to jump from his horse to catch a calf. The raised wooden heels would rest firmly in the stirrup while he was riding. Boot leather was thick - if a rattlesnake struck it, the fangs wouldn't

go in. Cowboys also wore metal spurs for nudging their horse to go faster. Leather 'chaps' covered their trousers, to protect them from underbrush or from the swinging horns of a frightened steer.

Being a cowboy was a hard, dangerous job. Cowboys (as well a few cowgirls!) could drown in a river, freeze in a blizzard or be crushed in a stampede. If a horse caught its foot in a prairie dog hole, it would go down and take the rider with it. The possibility of death was real, as seen in the words of a cowboy song:

> *O bury me not on the lone prairie*
> *Where the wild coyote will howl o'er me*
> *Where the buffalo roams the prairie sea*
> *O bury me not on the lone prairie.*

Many think of the cowboy on a cattle drive when they hear about the Wild West. Yet the drives lasted less than twenty years. Settlers began to fence in their land with barbed wire, and the railroad came to Texas. After that, cattle could be loaded on boxcars and ride to market. It was the end of the cowboy era. Nonetheless, there are plenty of cowboys around today. They still wear hats and boots and ride horses, even though 'driving' cattle means transporting them in a truck!

The Wild West cowboy had to occasionally fight Indians or chase cattle rustlers, but his life was not full of exciting adventures. He probably felt more like a slave than a king. Yet if he was lazy and slacked off, the cattle wouldn't be healthy. His job might have been boring, but it was an important one that needed to be done well.

Any time God gives you a job to do, it's an important one! He wants you to do it to the best of your ability even if it's boring. Maybe you think homework or household chores are dull. If you know God wants you to do a job well, that can make it easier to keep going, even when others don't notice what you're doing. Doing a task for God can even make it seem exciting!

And whatever you do or say, let it be as a representative of the Lord Jesus, all the while giving thanks through him to God the father. (Colossians 3:17)

Danger - White Water!

Oooooo! Ooooooo! We huddled together in our sleeping bags as the unearthly wail echoed through the still night air. It was our first night camping, near the banks of the Rio Grande in Big Bend National Park. We heard it again, a long chorus of ghostly voices.

'Coyotes!' my husband Roger said. 'Try to sleep - remember, we have to get up early tomorrow, to go white-water rafting.'

The coyotes were probably a few miles away, but their eerie howls bounced off the rocky cliff face behind us. It was a chilling, unforgettable sound, which would have been familiar to anyone living in the Wild West. The coyote (usually pronounced *KI-* yote or Ki-*YO*-tee) is a creature of legend, and many tall tales have been written about him. As settlers pushed across America, the native wolf population become smaller, so coyotes were free to spread far beyond their usual home west of the Mississippi River. Coyotes have been seen as far north as Alaska and as far east as Florida and New England. In 1995 a pair were found living in New York City!

A typical coyote looks like a slender gray dog. Like the British urban fox to which he is related, the coyote is a very adaptable creature. He is an omnivore, which means he will eat just about anything - grass, berries, insects, birds, mice, rabbits, leftovers in garbage cans - even the occasional small sheep or dog.

Scientists called 'scatologists' study the droppings or 'scat' of animals like the coyote, to discover what they have eaten. That is how we know so much about the eating habits of various animals - they leave behind a useful 'message' after their meals!

The next morning after we heard the coyotes howling, we woke up to a cold crisp November day with clear blue skies. We had been looking forward to our white-water rafting adventure for a long time. We had foolishly brought jackets padded with goose down - not a good idea for a trip down the river. If we got soaked, we'd end up wearing a heavy bag of wet feathers.

Arriving at the riverbank, we saw several large rubber rafts waiting for our group. Our guide, Greg, greeted us and handed each of us a bright orange life jacket. Roger and I along with our daughter Lisa climbed into the front of one raft while Greg sat in the middle with the oars. Three other passengers rode in the back. Greg pointed out the so-called 'chicken ropes' along the side of the raft, which we could grab onto if we were scared of falling overboard.

At first it was peaceful. We floated on the glassy river, gazing up at the patch of clear blue sky which seemed to grow smaller and smaller, as the high walls of the limestone canyon got closer together.

'Look, an eagle!' I called, seeing a large dark bird soaring overhead.

'No,' Greg said, 'that's a vulture. They do look like eagles because they are so big.'

Ugh! Instead of the grand eagle, we had seen the bald-headed bird which feeds on dead animals. However disgusting that sounds, the vulture performs an important task. It rids the desert of rotting animal corpses and its digestive system kills the bacteria as it passes through. You might call him the desert garbage collector! We were hoping to catch sight of other birds such as the peregrine falcon, a black and white bird about the size of a crow, which dives with amazing speed. However, they were more likely to be seen in the spring. More than 400 species of bird have been spotted in the Big Bend park. Suddenly we heard a loud roaring noise. 'Rapids ahead!' Greg called.

We rounded a bend to see the famous 'rock slide', formed centuries ago when part of the canyon collapsed, strewing the canyon with boulders the size of houses. We didn't think twice about clutching onto the 'chicken ropes'! The raft shot through the white water, plunging from left to right and back again as Greg guided the boat through the churning foam.

We made it! And our jackets were still mostly dry. The adventure was over quickly and now it was time for lunch, so the rafts docked at a level area of the canyon. Lisa and I wondered where the ladies' room was. We were startled to be handed a roll of toilet paper and pointed towards a large bush called the 'pink bush'! The men and boys were directed to the 'blue bush' on the opposite side of the area. Of course the bushes were not really pink or blue - this was just a nice way of saying, find a space to do your business, girls on one side and boys on the other.

White-water rafting is exciting and can be dangerous. Our trip turned out to be a lot of fun, but fairly tame - only our old tennis shoes got drenched. Danger from water for our family came later on another trip, on a river in central Texas.

Our youngest daughter, Millay, had several scary adventures with water during her childhood. Once when she was about three, she was leaning over looking into a large fish pond in front of a hotel when she fell in. We were thankful her older brother, David, was standing right there and pulled her out!

The most frightening incident happened when she was ten. Our family was 'tubing' down the Guadalupe River in central

Texas. Each person rode in their own large black tire tube. We drifted lazily down the river, enjoying the chilly water on a hot summer day. The adults lay on their backs but the children floated with their bodies inside the slippery tube hole, their arms hooked over one side. Everyone wore caps and tee shirts, and lots of waterproof sunscreen. We didn't want to come out at the end of the day looking like cooked lobsters! Little did we know there were other dangers we hadn't thought of.

Near the end of the tubing run, the river poured over a small dam or weir. That was the most exciting part of the trip! We were all laughing and joking as we sailed over the dam together. If we had known what was about to happen, we would have made sure we were holding on to the children's tubes.

At the foot of the dam where the rushing water fell, the river boiled and surged fiercely. I looked back to see Millay was in trouble! She had come out of her tube and was thrashing around

helplessly. Even though the water was shallow, she was gasping and choking as her head was held under the raging current.

'Help Millay!' I shouted to the others, as I let go of my tube and tried to force my way back upstream to her. But I couldn't buck the current quickly enough, and no one else was any closer to her.

Then out of the corner of my eye I saw a young man jump into the water from the bank. He waded swiftly across to Millay, pulled her out and held her safely until I could reach her. At that point I noticed the word on his baseball cap: *Lifeguard.*

He'd been there all the time, although I hadn't noticed him. He was watching and waiting for the moment when somebody needed him. Then he immediately came to the rescue. I thanked him, but was too shaken even to ask his name. Whoever he was, I am very grateful to that lifeguard!

The next morning we attended a local church. During the prayers I silently thanked God that our water adventure had not ended in tragedy. I was not prepared for what came next.

It was a small informal church, where people were encouraged to share answers to prayer. A man stood up and

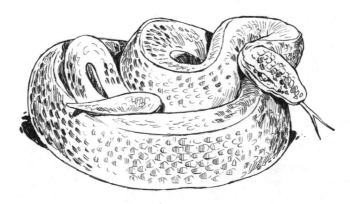

told us something that had happened as he was tubing down the Guadalupe River the day before, exactly where we had been.

He had been floating along lying on his back in his tube, wearing a large tee shirt to keep the sun off. The back of his shirt billowed out into the water. All of a sudden he felt something slide up under his shirt next to his bare back. He went very still. What was it? It was long and slender and smooth. A snake! Not only that, but he realized it was a cottonmouth, a snake which gets its name because its open mouth looks like it is filled with cotton. At that moment the man started praying, because the cottonmouth bite is poisonous. He was careful not to make any sudden moves and didn't tell his family what was happening. They splashed happily along, never realizing the danger their father was in.

The man told how he was finally able to slowly lift up the back of his tee shirt, and the cottonmouth swam away without biting him. Whew! Now we had two reasons to be thankful. We were really glad we hadn't heard that story *before* we went tubing!

I thought again of the lifeguard who had pulled Millay out of the river rapids. In a way, God's son, Jesus, is a lifeguard for us. He's the only one who can save us as we're paddling along in life, not realizing that the rapids are just ahead. We are just going our own way and not giving God much of a thought. We think we're 'not too bad' but God sees it differently.

So God sent his son, Jesus. When Jesus died on the cross, he took the punishment for every wrong thing we have ever done or thought. He made it possible for us to get to know God and belong to his family. Like the lifeguard, Jesus is right there when we call on him to save us.

What does God want you to do? Simply believe that Jesus is God's son and trust him to be your rescuer. God loves you very much, but you may not have been aware of that. He wants to take first place in your life. If you have not done so, you could pray to him and thank him for saving you. Praying simply means talking to God. You could use your own words or a prayer like this:

Dear God, thank you for sending your son, Jesus, to die on the cross for all the wrong things I have thought and said and done. Please forgive me and let me be in your family forever. Help me to be the kind of person you want me to be. Thank you for answering my prayer.

If you prayed that and meant it, then you are now a child of God. You don't need to keep on asking to become God's child - he heard you the first time! Since I am also his child, that means we now belong to the same family. I hope you will tell someone what you have done - perhaps a parent, or the person who gave you this book.

In other chapters, along with having Wild West adventures, we will learn some of the things that happen after a person has been forgiven by Jesus and begins to live as his follower. It promises to be an adventure even more exciting than white-water rafting!

And this is what God has testified: He has given us eternal life, and this life is in his Son. So whoever has God's son has life; whoever does not have his Son does not have life. (1 John 5:11-12)

Clones and Clever Critters

BAM! BAM! BAM! I curled up beneath the thin blanket, not daring to breathe as the heavy paw hit against our flimsy door.

'It's the bear!' whispered cousin Fay. She and her sister, Betsy, were in beds next to mine, in a wooden cabin in Sequoia National Park in California. Our families had driven here all the way from Texas, and we had persuaded our mothers to let us sleep in a cabin by ourselves.

'Can bears open doors?' I wondered. It was the middle of the night. We had been startled out of a sound sleep by a violent crashing outside. It was the bear destroying the metal cooler we had foolishly left out, and munching our leftover food. Apparently he was now looking for something more than just a snack – three terrified girls!

BAM! BAM! The bear didn't want to give up. I thought about the metal latch, which he could lift so easily with a flick of his paw. We lay as quietly as we could, trying not to whimper.

Suddenly Fay darted across the cold wooden floor in her bare feet. I heard the click of the bolt on the inside of the door and I dared to breathe again. Now, the bear could not simply walk in. He'd have to break the door down to get to us!

Finally the bear gave up and went away. The next morning when we came outside, we found the mangled remains of our cooler. That could have been one of us!

The black bear population declined in the early part of the 20th Century, as people hunted and trapped them in great numbers. But more bears have been sighted in recent years, in areas like Big Bend National Park in Texas. Normally a bear would not bother humans, but once it has tasted human food, it wants more. That can make it dangerous.

If you are in a National Park and see a bear, don't panic. Stay close together and give the bear plenty of room. Don't hang around too long, and never get between a mother bear and her cubs!

Not all animals in the Wild West are big and scary - one is small, feathered and funny looking. The roadrunner is a brave and adaptable bird with an oversized beak and long tail. He has speckled black and white feathers and bright red and blue skin around the eyes. The crest on his head pops up and down like a flag.

Is the roadrunner coming or going? Who knows! If you are trying to figure this out from its tracks, you may be confused, as two of his toes point forwards and two backwards. No matter where he's headed, he's in a hurry. This little desert bird runs about fifteen miles (twenty-four kilometers) per hour, which most humans would find hard to beat! Some Indians had a legend that eating roadrunner meat would help them run swiftly.

The roadrunner is active in all seasons. In summer he is able to squeeze his feathers together to keep out the scorching heat. Can you imagine not drinking a drop of anything, on even the hottest day? Well, the roadrunner doesn't! He gets all the moisture he needs from food. In winter he will turn his back to the sun and raise his feathers to let the sun get down onto his skin. The black skin quickly soaks up the heat, and the bird warms up.

Roadrunners are also clever in keeping the size of their brood low when there is a drought and food is scarce. In those years, the female simply doesn't lay any eggs. She will wait another year to have her family.

What does this plucky bird eat? Just about anything, including small rattlesnakes! The roadrunner will circle around a snake, pretending to be harmless. When the rattler strikes, the roadrunner leaps back to avoid being hit and then darts forward, grabbing the snake and tossing it into the air. When it lands, he bites it on the head and bangs it to death on a nearby rock. If the snake is long, the roadrunner leaves part of it hanging out of his beak until his stomach has room to digest it!

Extreme climates like the desert demand that an animal be able to fit in with the surroundings in order to survive. Unlike the roadrunner, many creatures hide in their burrows during the day and keep the entrance covered up so the air inside stays cool. You probably know that animals like these which come out only at night are called 'nocturnal'.

(A tip: in hot weather you may be more likely to see animals in the wild near sunrise or sundown; in cold weather, they will be most active in the afternoon.)

Animals are not the only desert creatures designed to stand a harsh climate. Did you know that plants can get sunburn? They don't use sunscreen, but they have other ways of dealing with the searing desert heat. Cacti have a tough skin with a waxy coating which keeps sun out and moisture in. Their prickly spines don't evaporate water like the leaves on other plants, and they store up water inside their thick spongy stems. Their roots are shallow but wide, so that they can quickly suck up any rain that might fall.

But they have an even more remarkable trick for dealing with the heat – waiting! The seeds of many desert plants ignore a rainfall and refuse to sprout, unless the rain is heavy enough to see the new plant through its whole life cycle. Just as the roadrunner can wait to have its young, the seeds of certain plants can wait for a year or two, until the rainfall is greater. Then the new plants will be sure to survive and produce other plants.

Waiting is a good trick for humans to learn, too. Sometimes we think we must have something *right now* – but if we grab for what we want too soon, it may be the wrong time for it. We might miss the good that would come from waiting until the right time. Do you find it hard to wait for something good to come – a birthday, a special treat, maybe even being old enough to eat what you want when you want, or to drive a car? I find waiting difficult too.

But God says it is good to wait – if we are waiting for *him*. We may be hoping for something or even asking God for it, and not seeing it happen. He might be saying 'No, that would not be something good for you to have.' On the other hand, he could be saying 'Wait – trust me – you will see what I will do, in my own time.' When we learn to wait like that, we are living by faith instead of by our feelings or what we can see. That makes God happy!

Along with plants that know how to wait, the West has some plants and animals that can make exact copies of themselves. These are called clones. In the West, one aspen tree growing next to another is very likely its clone. Huge groves of these slender trees with their white trunks and shimmering leaves are all part of one plant. They look identical because they are! They are the same height and thickness, and their leaves turn color at exactly the same time in the autumn.

In western Colorado there are groves of aspen containing millions of trees - all clones with identical genes. This helps them fight back when forest fires strike. Their roots can quickly send up new shoots, to create a forest where one was destroyed.

Cloning in nature is a good idea. But I would not want to be a human clone, would you? What if there were another person on the earth who is your exact double - someone who is like you in every detail? You might be walking down the street and meet 'yourself' coming the other way! Yet no one on earth is exactly like you. Even twins may look very similar, but they are two different people, with different fingerprints and each with their own personality.

Each person on the earth is created by God and loved by him. We are not just a mass of humans to him. He wants each one of us to get to know him personally. Did you know that God was watching over you even before you were born? He knows the exact number of hairs on your head. Whether you are having a bad day or a good one, God knows all about it. Thank him that you are not a clone, but a dearly loved person who is very special to him.

Thank you for making me so wonderfully complex! Your workmanship is marvelous - and how well I know it. You watched me as I was being formed in utter seclusion, as I was woven together in the dark of the womb. (Psalm 139:14-15)

People of the Buffalo

It was a warm spring day in East Texas, 1836. The white settlers of Fort Parker left the gate of their wooden stockade open while they worked in the nearby fields. That was a mistake.

A group of Indians from the Comanche and Kiowa tribes approached carrying a white flag and asking for beef. Then suddenly, the Indians stormed the stockade and killed five settlers. Before young Cynthia Ann Parker knew what was happening, she was strapped to a Comanche horse by one of the warriors, her blonde hair flying out behind her as they galloped away.

Often when the Indians raided, it was in revenge for an injury done to them. No matter if the whites they killed were not the ones who had killed their people, they paid back death for death, murdering whole families. Cynthia Ann must have seen the Indians kill her father and other relatives. She knew she would either be tortured and killed, or else kept and raised as one of the Comanche. She could only hope and pray and wait.

Imagine how strange it must have felt - a young girl who knew only English, used to the white way of living, suddenly surrounded by Comanche jabbering in a foreign language, talking about her. What were they saying? Perhaps she stared closely at the expression on each person's face, trying to read kindness there. They would have stared back, fascinated by her blue eyes and blonde hair.

What would her fate be? As it turned out, Cynthia was allowed to live. The Comanche adopted her and gave her a new name. They were one of the tribes which lived on the Great Plains which covered the central part of America. Cynthia's life would never be the same.

In her early days at the Indian's camp even the smells would have been so different from anything she had known before. First there was the smell of bear fat which the people rubbed onto their skin and hair. Then there was the smell of buffalo (actually a bison, not related to the water buffalo). The Indians used every part of the buffalo either for food or tools or clothing or shelter. They even melted buffalo fat and drank it!

Cynthia's new home was not a log cabin but instead a large tepee of tanned buffalo hide where all the members of her Comanche family slept. She would become skillful at the tedious women's task of scraping the hair and flesh from a dried buffalo hide, using a tool made from buffalo bone. She would learn how to rub a mixture of animal brains into the hide, to cure it and make it soft. She would be taught to ride a horse bareback, to eat pemmican (a kind of sausage) and to start a fire using pieces of wood.

Here is a recipe for pemmican, in case you happen to have some buffalo meat:

1. Cut slices of buffalo meat and hang them on a rack in the sun.
2. When the meat is very dry, pound it with a stone to make a powder.
3. Mix the powder with melted buffalo fat. Add some wild berries.
4. Take some cleaned-out buffalo intestines, and stuff the mixture inside.
5. Store in a 'parfleche', a decorated bag made of skin.

Pemmican will keep for a couple of years without spoiling.

The Plains Indians had followed this way of life ever since the Spaniards brought horses to America on their ships in the 1500's. Before that, they had to hunt the mighty buffalo on foot! The best way of hunting in those days was to cause a stampede near the edge of a cliff. The beasts would plunge to the bottom, and it was up to the hunters waiting below to kill them with spears or bow and arrow.

Once horses arrived, the Indians began to depend on them for everything. If you were a boy, you began learning to ride a horse when you were very young. Sometimes a father would strap his toddler securely to the back of a horse, and away he'd go! You would have been riding from the time you could walk.

Then when you were old enough, you would be allowed to go on a buffalo hunt! Your father would make you ride behind him at first, for safety. The men on horseback would surround a herd so the buffalo would be confused and not know which way to run. You would watch very carefully as your father maneuvered his horse close enough to one buffalo. He would try to take it down with one or two arrows straight into the heart, because a furious wounded buffalo could be deadly.

The hunter's horse had to be very fast and agile. It could weave in and out like magic, not even needing the rider to tell it what to do. There was often a piece of leather dangling from the bridle which the hunter could grab if he fell off.

Your father took aim and let his arrow fly. The buffalo was down! The whole tribe including children ran quickly to gut and skin the dead beasts. The hunters took their prize - the steaming raw liver eaten on the spot, maybe sprinkled with green bile from the gall bladder. Delicious - or so they say! As you helped to peel the skin from the buffalo's flesh, you would feel proud that your father was a skillful hunter, but also anxious to be old enough to kill a buffalo yourself.

The family was very important to tribal life and each person had a part to play. Boys were trained by their fathers in the exciting tasks of riding, shooting with bow and arrow, spears or guns, and hunting. It was their job to feed and protect their relatives when they grew up. Girls learned to ride as well, but their main tasks were in handicrafts and homemaking. They were taught by their mothers how to gather fruits and berries, cook, sew, make tepees, tan buffalo hides. In tribes which depended on farming, that work was done entirely by the women.

The huge tepees were sewn together out of twelve or more buffalo hides, using bird or animal bones for needles. At the top was an opening for the smoke to escape, with flaps to close when it rained. The women and girls not only sewed the tepee, they would build it, pulling the hides over a cone-shaped frame of poles tied together at the top. And they were the ones to take the tepee down when it was time to move camp.

It was a busy life, yet the children had time to play. They enjoyed games similar to hockey, lacrosse and soccer, using a rawhide ball stuffed with moss. They also played games with dice.

The Plains Indians believed in a spirit force of Nature which lived in the sun, earth, moon, sky, wind, water and animals. They would pray to the spirits of the buffalo and other creatures which they hunted. Even so they sometimes killed far more many buffalo than they needed.

Christians do not pray to Nature, yet we often need to learn greater respect for God's creation. In our modern world we can get cut off from the earth and its beauty. God gave us this world to take care of. Instead of being caretakers as he intended, sometimes we are vandals, wasting what he has given. When we mistreat his gift, it is an insult to the giver.

Is there something you can do to make a difference to how we treat Nature? Perhaps you could put out feeders for wild creatures, recycle more, or even write a letter to your local newspaper. Ask your family to help you think of ways that together you can be better caretakers of God's creation.

It may sound as if the women did most of the work in the tribe. Yet in addition to trading as well as hunting, the Plains Indian men had another essential task: warfare. Tribes would often steal horses from each other, or carry out raids. Warriors had to be ready at all times to defend their people to the death. Boys as young as thirteen would go along on raids, learning the ways of war.

Much of their time was spent in preparing weapons. Each warrior painted his arrows with his own markings, so it was clear after a battle or hunt which kill was his. They made shields from the thick hump skin of a buffalo and painted them with special symbols. The shield would not only stop arrows but was also thought to have spiritual power.

Even their horses would be painted with signs from Nature or the spirit world, which the warriors believed would protect them in battle. It was considered a major honor in battle to take an enemy's horse or gun or scalp. Sometimes they would just touch an armed enemy without harming him, to show how brave they were.

You may wonder, why did these trained warriors let the whites take their land? But the Indians didn't see the land as something to be owned. Most didn't think of the white man as a real threat. The Plains tribes were nomadic, which means they moved around and hunted their food rather than farming. They wanted the freedom to roam and hunt as they had always done, and did not understand that once the West was settled and divided up, that freedom would disappear.

The Plains Indians could not imagine that the vast herds of buffalo which they needed for survival, would one day be gone. But as more and more people headed West, buffalo and other wild game were hunted so much that they became scarce. After the Civil War, the Texas government slaughtered thousands of the great beasts, leaving their carcasses to rot on the Plains. They were hoping to starve out the Indians by taking away their main source of food and clothing.

Sadly, it worked. The buffalo numbers went from millions down to just a few hundred by 1900. Also, the 'open range' was no longer open. The invention of barbed wire in 1873 meant settlers could fence off the land, so animals and people could not roam freely.

Some Indian chiefs realized that the only way their tribes would survive, would be to stop fighting the whites, sign a treaty and move to plots of land called 'reservations'. There they would have to learn to farm or raise cattle instead of hunting as they had always done. As he signed such a treaty in 1867, the Comanche Chief Ten Bears said, 'I do not want

the churches and the houses. I was born on the prairie where the wind blew free and there was nothing to break the light of the sun... we only wish to wander over the prairie until we die.'

Another famous Comanche chief who signed a treaty was Quanah Parker. Remember Cynthia Ann, kidnapped by the Comanche? Quanah was her son. He was a fierce warrior, but he finally surrendered in 1875 and became chief of the Comanche reservation in Oklahoma. After that, he worked hard to help save his people's lands.

Cynthia was re-captured by the Texas Rangers when Quanah was about fifteen. But she had lived too long as a Comanche. She tried in vain to escape back to her tribe. She was never happy living with the Parker family, trying to fit into white people's ways.

Today there are more buffalo than at the end of the Wild West. They live on game ranches or in wildlife refuges. Instead of its role in life of the Indian, the buffalo now has a starring role in movies! However, care is taken that no animals (or people!) are harmed. In

Dances with Wolves, any dead buffalo you see are made of latex. In that movie when a buffalo charges at a young Indian girl, he is actually a tame beast who is coming towards her to get a cookie!

More than 500 Indian tribal groups are officially recognized in the US today, many still living on reservation land with tribal government as the local authority. They often prefer being called 'a member of the Comanche (or whichever) tribe' rather than 'Native American' or 'American Indian'. They wear modern clothing and work at typical jobs. Yet for many the traditional rituals and costumes are still very important. The Plains Indians meet together in 'pow-wows', times for dancing, feasting and keeping their customs alive.

Not all American Indians follow the traditional ways of their religion. Many have become followers of Jesus. They still have great respect for their heritage, but instead of worshipping the creation, they worship the God who made it.

Many people think that all religions are the same - that they are all different ways of getting to know God - yet that is not the case. Most religions teach that you should try to be kind and unselfish. But that can be very hard to do! Being a follower of Jesus does not mean struggling to follow religious rules. Instead of just trying really hard to be good, I can ask Jesus to help me. He doesn't want me to follow a set of rules, but to live in close friendship with him every day.

(Jesus said) 'I no longer call you servants, because a master doesn't confide in his servants. Now you are my friends, since I have told you everything the Father told me.' (John 15:15)

The Journey Westward

Ma! Look - there's a piano lying right next to the trail! Can we take it with us?'

'I'm sorry, dear - I know you hated to leave your piano behind in Kentucky. But where would we put it?'

'Well then, if we can't take the piano, can I at least ride in the wagon? My feet hurt!'

'I'm afraid we'll just have to keep on walking. Our poor oxen can barely pull the wagon as it is!'

The pioneer family had left their home and most of their possessions behind, when they headed West. Sometimes people tried to take too much with them, and found that their wagon was too heavy for their oxen to pull. The pathways to the West such as the famous Oregon Trail were scattered with bits of furniture that had to be abandoned - an early form of litter!

The typical means of transport was the 'prairie schooner', a cloth-covered wagon that looked like a ship sailing out on the waving 'sea' of prairie grass. This cart which was only about ten feet (three meters) long had to carry everything the travelers would use on a five-month long journey, plus what they would need to set up home in the wilderness. It was much smaller than the average caravan or motor home seen on the road today. There was not much room inside for pianos or people!

The wagon was perfectly designed for the task. It was light enough to be pulled by a team of oxen and its wide wheels rolled easily over the rough trails. Here were some of the things you might see inside a covered wagon: blankets, feather duvets, rifles, pistols, knives, hatchet, gunpowder, coffee, flour, salt, corn meal, dried beans, dried fruit, rice, boots, sunbonnets, ax, hammer, hoe, plow, shovel, whetstone, ropes, china, school books, dolls, plant cuttings, kettle, skillet, coffee grinder, coffee pot, water keg, matches, surgical instruments, bandages, scissors, sewing kit, chamber pot. How many of these do you have in your house today?

Imagine what it was like. You are walking along in the blazing sun, next to the sweating flank of a sturdy ox as it slowly plods through the wilderness. There is nothing to see but the wide blue sky above and the tall prairie grass on either side of the trail. You hear the snorts of the oxen, the creak of the wagon wheels, the constant hum of the wind singing through the long grass. Your whole family is walking. There's no room in the wagon, and horses would have been too expensive to feed on the harsh trail. The oxen are slow but they don't need much food, and your father will use them to pull the plow when you reach your new home.

'Are we there yet?' Hopefully the children didn't say that every five minutes for the whole five months!

'We'll make camp before sundown - still a ways to go today, and many more days after that!'

'Pa, I can't see Johnny! He was right here a moment ago!'

'Quick - climb onto the wagon and see if you can spot him!'

'There he is, right in the middle of that tall grass! Johnny! Get back over here right now - the Indians will get you!'

'Better let him ride up in the wagon for a while. We'd never find him if he wandered very far.'

It was important to stay close to the wagon. The land on the Great Plains was flat or slightly rolling, covered with grass known as 'tallgrass'. In summer it could reach up to the height of a one-story building. You could easily lose a cow, not to mention a child! And there were Indians, although many were friendly and just wanted to trade with the pioneers. The settlers traveled in large groups and circled up the wagons every night for safety.

Later settlers were able to take the stagecoach all the way across America. Although faster than the covered wagon, this was a rough journey as the stagecoach was nothing more than an enclosed box pulled by a team of horses. Before heading out West in the stagecoach travelers may have read these useful tips:

- The best seat is next to the driver. You will get less than half of the bumps and jolts there.

- Never ride in extremely cold weather - you might freeze to death!

- Don't wear tight-fitting shoes or gloves. Your feet and hands will likely swell in the heat, and you won't be able to get your shoes off. Bathe your feet and hands in cold water before you set out.

- Don't grease your hair. Dust from the road will settle on it and it will look like you powdered it.

- If the horses bolt, just sit tight and take your chances. If you jump off, you're more likely to be hurt.

- Don't smoke a strong pipe, especially early in the morning. If you have to spit, do it on the leeward side (the opposite side from which the wind is blowing), so your spit doesn't fly back onto you or your fellow passengers.

* Don't swear, or lop over onto your neighbor while sleeping.
* Never fire a gun on the road - it may frighten the horses.
* Don't point out places on the road where horrible murders have taken place.
* Don't ask how far it is to the next station.

(Adapted from 'Hints for Plains Travelers' published in the Omaha Herald, 1877)

No matter whether you went by stagecoach or covered wagon, it was a long and weary journey. What a relief when you finally heard the shout, 'We're here!'

When the settlers arrived at their destination, for example the fertile and beautiful Willamott Valley in Oregon territory, it must have looked like paradise. Perhaps it will be a bit like that for Christians, when they leave their homes on this earth and pass through death to the place of amazing beauty which is Heaven. The Bible describes Heaven as a real physical place and says that those who trust in Jesus Christ will have new bodies when they get there. It won't be just a place of spirits floating around on clouds. We will have work to do there and many adventures wait for us.

Jesus told his followers that he was going ahead of them, to get their special new home ready. What a great day that will be, when God's children arrive at their new home and see the Lord Jesus standing there with open arms welcoming them. They will be even more joyful than the weary travelers from the Wild West!

But let's get back to the prairie - we've still got more discoveries to make. Although it may look dull and flat, the prairie teems with life. Whatever lives on the prairie has to be able to stand the extreme heat and cold, drought, tornados and blizzards of the Great Plains. The prairie has its own unique 'ecosystem' - the place where a wide variety of plants and animals all support each other.

An excellent example of the prairie ecosystem is the prairie dog. This chubby member of the squirrel family tunnels underground to make its burrows. Prairie dogs come out during the day, often standing on the mound of their hole and peering around looking for predators such as hawks, coyotes or bobcats. They keep the area around the burrow entrance cleared of grass so they can easily spot danger. If they see something coming, the prairie dogs hop up and down and make high-pitched barking sounds, then dive into their burrows.

Ever since the West was settled farmers and ranchers have trapped or shot prairie dogs, fearing their cattle will step into the holes and break a leg. They also worry that the prairie dog will eat all the grass meant for the cattle. Actually, the prairie dog tunnels improve the soil, and their grazing makes new grass grow. They also have their own way of dealing with overpopulation - eating their own newborn young!

Sometimes it becomes necessary to 'relocate' the prairie dogs, to move them to a different site to make way for a housing development. This may be done by flushing the burrows with water - the escaping animals are then trapped and carried to a place where empty burrows are ready for them to move into. In other cases the prairie dogs are sucked up by a giant vacuum cleaner on a truck and then carried away to be spewed out somewhere else. Neither of these methods is much fun for the animals and many of them don't live through it.

The prairie dog is called a 'keystone species' for the prairies. This means that if they are removed, many other forms of life will die out. For example, prairie dogs move house every so often, when their own becomes too infested with fleas. When they go, other animals move in. The vacant burrows provide homes for animals such as burrowing owls, black-footed ferrets and snakes. (A tip: NEVER stick your hand down a burrow to see what's living there. You could get a nasty surprise!)

The prairie dog also provides food for coyotes, badgers and many birds of prey. Over 200 other species have been seen living near prairie dog colonies.

Wherever there is a balanced 'ecosystem' or habitat, if one part is taken away the whole structure gets off balance and may collapse and disappear. This is true for the animal kingdom and for the earthly Christian 'kingdom' as well! A group of Christians who worship together is called a 'body'. Just as a body has many necessary parts, so each individual Christian is a necessary part of the whole. If you stub your big toe your whole body notices it. If it's bleeding, your brain will tell your feet and hands to move quickly to get something to bandage it.

You may not feel that you are a very important part of your church or youth group. But God says you are! You could do without your big toe if you had to, but you wouldn't want to. If it were missing, your whole body would be thrown out of line. In the same way, you have an vital part to play in the Christian 'body'. Just as the prairie dog is a keystone species, each one of us is a keystone person.

Every Christian is able to do something that benefits the church as a whole. It may be something like helping others by doing something practical for them, or encouraging those who are feeling down, or inviting people into your home and making them feel welcome. The Bible lists over a dozen spiritual gifts - abilities that God has given to those who believe in him. You may have no idea what your gift is, but the best way to find out is to start trying things out. Ask God to give you an idea of something you could do for someone this week.

Just as our bodies have many parts and each part has a special function, so it is with Christ's body. We are all parts of his one body, and each of us has different work to do. And since we are all one body in Christ, we belong to each other, and each of us needs all the others.' (Romans 12:4-5)

The Gun that Won the West

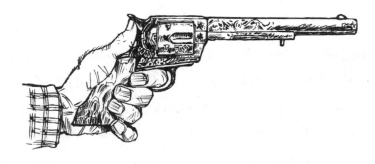

The scene was the town square in Springfield, Missouri, in the year 1865. After an argument over a card game, gambler Dave Tutt and 'Wild Bill' Hickok decided to duel. They faced off at opposite ends of the street and began walking towards each other. When they were about fifty paces apart Hickok hollered, 'Don't come any closer, Dave!' Both men drew their guns. Tutt quickly fired and missed. Hickok aimed his gun carefully and shot Tutt right through the heart.

You may be surprised to learn that this was one of the few recorded 'draw and shoot' duels in the Wild West. It was not that easy to aim a pistol drawn quickly from the hip. A gunslinger would be more likely to have his weapon ready before he entered a dangerous situation. And he tried to make sure the other man didn't draw first. The only rule was, don't shoot an unarmed man.

Although most of the West was untamed territory, towns sprang up overnight after gold and silver were discovered, as people hurried westward to try and make a quick fortune. Other towns grew up around the last stops on the railroad line, while still others were 'cowtowns' where the cattle trails ended.

Many of these places had no official law and order, and groups called 'vigilantes' ruled instead. That meant they were vigilant or on the alert for any crime, which they might punish by hanging on the spot. This would often gruesomely be referred to as a 'necktie party'. Vigilante groups were formed with good intentions but they often turned violent and did more damage than they prevented.

The West was full of wild, lawless men. Jesse James and his brother, Frank, became leaders of a band of outlaws, and were famous even in their own time. Billy the Kid had already been in prison by the age of sixteen and killed his first man two years later. He himself was shot and killed when he was only twenty-two. Other well-known outlaws were an Indian scout named Apache Kid, Doc Holliday who was a dentist turned gambler and gunfighter, and many more.

Even while they were alive, romantic and colorful stories were written about many of these outlaws, making them out to be much more generous and noble than was the case. For example, tales were spread that Frank and Jesse James robbed from the rich to give to the poor, but that may have been a story made up by their mother! The truth was often much more grim: men shot and killed others for nothing more serious than to settle an argument. Instead of understanding that life is a precious gift from God, they would snuff it out as if it was worthless.

What kind of lawmen could stand up to hardened killers like these? Some of the more famous ones were in Dodge City, Kansas, known as one of the most violent towns in the West. There was Marshal Bill Tilghman, who never drew his gun unless he had to, as well as Bat Masterson, who also helped to bring the law into the towns of Tombstone, Arizona and Deadwood, South Dakota.

One of the most legendary lawmen was Wyatt Earp who was assistant marshal in Dodge, where he became friends with Doc Holliday. Wyatt wore a special long overcoat and always kept his pistol in his coat pocket, which he had

lined with canvas and wax to make it easy to draw. He took his time aiming, and usually only pulled the trigger once.

Killings often took place out of revenge, when tempers were hot. It was not easy to figure out who was in the wrong. Lawmen might help restore order to one town, then go on to murder people themselves. When Wild Bill Hickok was marshal of Abilene, Kansas, he was able to disarm gunslinger John Wesley Hardin and run him out of town. That same year, Hickok accidentally shot and killed a deputy marshal. Hickok died in a poker game with a bullet in his back, shot in revenge for another killing. He made the mistake of sitting with his back to the door that one time, and it cost him his life.

Although many people did not carry guns, those who did had their favorites. The most popular rifle was the Winchester '73, known as the 'gun that won the West'. It held fifteen rounds of ammunition. Each bullet would be pushed into the breech by cranking the trigger guard forward and back. This was called a 'lever action' rifle. It certainly beat having to stop and take a minute or two before loading each charge, as was the case with

the Kentucky rifle of the early pioneer days. Rifles could fire at a long range with accuracy, although not from a galloping horse!

Probably more people were killed in the Wild West with the Colt six-shooter, originally called the 'Peacemaker'. Unlike earlier revolvers which had to be loaded with gunpowder and then the ball of the bullet, the Peacemaker used 'fixed' metal bullets containing the powder, percussion cap and ball in one casing. Its cylinder held six bullets. The Peacemaker did bring peace, in a way, but by death. Lives were cut short, often over something as trivial as a card game or insult.

Like the Winchester, the Colt revolver has also been called the 'gun that won the West'. It is said that there were as many revolvers as men in Texas during that time.

Jesus taught his followers, 'Blessed are the peacemakers.' What do you think he meant? He certainly was not talking about using guns! Can you think of better ways to bring peace into a troubled situation? Jesus is called the 'Prince of Peace'. He wants to bring his peace into homes and neighborhoods and schools, beginning with you and me.

One important part of peace is *forgiveness*. We will get stuck in our friendship with Jesus if we refuse to forgive someone, even if the other person is in the wrong. Jesus will still love us, but we will be like a child sitting in a corner clutching an old broken toy, when Jesus wants us to let go of it so he can give us a new one.

The first step in forgiving is to ask Jesus' forgiveness for anything you know you have done wrong. It's a good idea to do that as soon as you are aware of anything that you know would not make him happy. Then thank him that he has forgiven you. He promised he would, and he will keep his promise!

Next, is there someone you are finding it hard to forgive? Ask Jesus to help you. You may need to go to the person and say a sincere 'sorry' for your part in the problem. This isn't easy, but you could pray with another Christian, that Jesus will help you spread his peace by forgiving others.

One of the most notorious criminals of the Wild West was John Wesley Hardin, son of a Methodist preacher in Texas. At the age of fifteen he killed a man in revenge for being beaten in a fight. He had such a bad reputation by the age of sixteen that the Governor of Texas vowed to have him murdered, jailed or hung. Yet his friends and family always protected him. Finally the Texas Rangers captured him and he served nineteen years in prison, trying in vain to escape many times.

Hardin seemed to be reformed when he first came out of prison, but his quick temper continued to stir up trouble. He was eventually shot by a sheriff in a saloon, because he made rude remarks

about the sheriff's son. In all, Hardin probably killed between thirty and forty people, more than any other Wild West outlaw.

We were surprised to discover, when going through some papers related to my husband's family, that one of his grandmothers had the last name of Hardin before she married. We also found other documents about the outlaw John Wesley Hardin. Was he one of my husband's ancestors? We have not yet discovered the connection, but we did find out that the family 'tree' includes a cattle thief by the name of Injun Joe Vann!

That may sound like a terrible heritage, but does it matter? No. As a follower of Jesus, it's not so important where you have

come from - the main question is, where are you headed? Will you help others or harm them, like the outlaws we've heard about? Perhaps you will have children yourself someday, although that may sound like a long way off. What kind of teaching and example will you pass on to them?

No matter what your background is, you have a choice of which path to follow, and you don't have to walk it alone. When you give your life to Jesus, he comes and lives in you and makes you fresh and new. You are still yourself, but with a big difference - Jesus. If you belong to Jesus and are walking with him, your life can be a blessing for all who know you and for generations after you.

...those who become Christians become new persons. They are not the same anymore, for the old life is gone. A new life has begun! (2 Corinthians 5:17)

Famous or Faithful?

What's wrong with that man's face?' asked the little girl.

'Hush!' whispered her mother. 'He's been in an accident. Don't stare - it's not polite!'

In spite of her mother's warning, the little girl couldn't help gazing up at the stagecoach driver. He was small, with the leathery sun-baked skin of a driver and a cigar clamped in his teeth. It was the ugly scar across his eye that caught the girl's attention.

Except for the scar, a result of being kicked in the face by a horse, Charley Parkhurst was no different from the typical stagecoach driver. He had muscular arms and scarred hands from handling the reins of six horses plus a whip. For twenty years he drove the dangerous route over the Sierra Nevada mountains in California, until he retired and opened a saloon around 1870.

But Charley had a secret, one which would cause him to become famous all over America after his death.

Another Wild Westerner who became famous after death was Belle Starr, who died at age forty from a gunshot wound in the back. Even during her lifetime many romantic stories were told about this woman who stole horses and was glad to hide people who were on the run from 'the law'. In the stories she was called the beautiful 'Bandit Queen', but those who knew her described her as 'bony and flat-chested with a mean mouth'.

Calamity Jane was a western woman who lived up to her nickname - she brought trouble to anyone who tried to trouble her! Jane was an adventurous girl who learned to ride a horse at an early age. On her family's journey westward she would ride back and forth across raging streams swollen with rain, just for the fun of it. While still in her teens she used coarse language, drank whiskey and began wearing men's clothes.

Pretty soon she was a well-known character. It is not known whether Calamity Jane ever shot anyone, but the story is told that when some cowboys in a saloon were jeering at her, she whipped out two revolvers and made them dance to dodge the bullets. She wrote in her autobiography that by the age of twenty she was considered 'the most reckless and daring rider and one of the best shots in the western country.' When she came to Deadwood, South Dakota at the age of twenty-four, the local newspaper reported 'Calamity Jane has arrived'.

'Little Sure Shot' was a tiny woman better known to us as Annie Oakley. Born in a log cabin in Ohio, Annie began shooting game at age nine to help feed her family. By the time she was twelve, she could shoot the head off of a running quail. When Annie was sixteen she won a shooting contest against Frank E. Butler, who later married her. They traveled around the country giving shows, and eventually joined the famous Buffalo Bill Wild West Show.

Annie became the show's star and her fame with both rifle and six-gun spread. She could hit the edge of a playing card tossed in the air at ninety feet (twenty-seven meters). In one day using a .22 rifle she shot 4,472 of 5,000 glass balls which were thrown in the air. One of her favorite tricks was shooting the ashes off of a cigarette in Frank's mouth.

Sacajawea was another western woman, famous for her part in the Lewis and Clark expedition to the Pacific Ocean in the early 1800's. She was not an official member of the group nor did she lead Lewis and Clarke, as some believe. Her husband had been hired as an interpreter and she was allowed to come along. She was able to interpret for them when they encountered Shoshone-speaking Indians.

Although she was only sixteen years old, Sacajawea was praised by the men of the expedition for her calmness in the face of danger. They were sailing on the Missouri River when they were hit by a sudden storm. Their boat keeled over on its side and nearly capsized. With her three-month-old baby strapped to her back, Sacajawea moved quickly and calmly to gather up the books and instruments that started to float away in the choppy water. Many valuable items would have been lost, except for her cool head.

By now, perhaps you have guessed the secret of stagecoach driver Charley Parkhurst. It was not discovered until he died and was examined by a doctor. The tough, rough-living Charley was a woman! Apparently Charley had run away from home as a child and become a stable boy. She had stayed in the man's world ever since. She was described as shy and probably would have been very upset about the fame that came to her after her death. In those days, people were shocked that a woman could do such a grueling job and pretend for so long to be a man.

When God made people, the Bible tells us, he created them 'male and female', saying that he made them 'in his image'.

Whether you are a boy or a girl, God loves you very much and regards you as equally special. Yet he also wants you to understand that there are things about your gender (in other words, your being male or female) that are unique. You didn't end up being a boy or a girl by accident - it was part of God's design for you. Thank God that he made you the gender that you are.

Most women of the West never became famous. They came from many different races and language groups, to join their husbands on the hard trek to the wilderness. Once they got there, they had to struggle to raise their children and farm untamed land.

The flat, treeless prairie where some families settled didn't offer a lot of materials to build houses. Their first home would be in an underground dug-out, or one made of sod bricks cut out of the hard ground. They would take the canvas from the covered wagon and string it over the ceiling, to keep bugs and dirt in the roof from falling into the one room.

The nearest neighbor might be two days' journey away. The pioneer home had to be self-sufficient - everything they ate had to be grown on their land or hunted, except for a few special items like sugar or white flour, which they would buy at the nearest store two or three times a year.

The early pioneer wife made clothes for the whole family, often from home-grown cotton. Children would help water and hoe the cotton, and pick the fluffy balls from the plants which had fierce spines. Then they would 'gin' it by picking out the seeds and 'card' it before spinning it into thread on a

spinning wheel. After that, it was woven into cloth on a loom. The finished cloth was dyed using whatever they had: dark blue dye from a boiled indigo plant, or brown dye from walnuts or even from dirt.

Most people only had one outfit to wear, so they didn't wash their clothes very often. If everyone smelled the same, I guess no one noticed! A man usually only had one pair of trousers. If they got torn, he had to go to bed while his wife stitched them up!

The wife was also the family doctor. She had a list of home remedies, including making her children eat well-roasted mouse if they had the measles. She would put coal oil on their scalp to cure dandruff. There were no hospitals in the wilderness, and a wife would have her babies at home, helped by a neighbor or her husband.

On top of all that, the pioneer woman had to help with the farming, bake bread, cook everything without any help from a supermarket, make her own candles and soap, and be able to protect the home against Indians when her husband was out hunting. She would also teach her children at home, if no school was nearby.

All in all, the pioneer wife had a hard and lonely life, in the days before there were enough settlers to make up a town. Most of these women were not known outside the circle of their own family. Often they had a strong faith in God, yet they did not always have the benefit of being able to worship in a church. Instead, the family would pray and worship God together. These women kept on faithfully doing what they had to, to make the wilderness a home.

Of course, the children had to work hard too. They did pretty much everything their parents did, whether milking the cows, gathering eggs, baking bread or helping sew and mend the family's clothing. Still, they could find a bit of time to play hopscotch or leapfrog or marbles, and the occasional local dance would provide a real treat.

One pioneer woman only became famous because her daughter insisted that she write down the stories of her childhood in the West. That woman was Laura Ingalls Wilder, who wrote the *Little House on the Prairie* books. Her detailed stories give a vivid picture of what it was like to be growing up at that time.

Do you ever dream about how nice it would be, to be famous? Would you like to have everyone know your name and recognize you wherever you go? More important than being famous is being faithful, just as many pioneer women were, and just as God is all the time. He proves it by never giving up on us.

For you, being faithful could mean finishing a job someone is expecting you to do, or keeping a promise you have made even when it is hard, or patiently loving someone who is difficult. It also means doing the best you can with the personality and talents you have, instead of trying to be someone you're not.

You may never become famous, but God will notice. Whether boy or girl, you can be faithful in using well the talents and abilities he has given. That's better than having your name go down in history!

The master said, 'Well done, my good and faithful servant. You have been faithful in handling this small amount, so now I will give you many more responsibilities. Let's celebrate together!' (Matthew 25:23)

Come 'n Get It!

A lone bird chirps in the darkness. There is a faint hint of dawn. 'Cookie', as the men call him, is already up. He picks his way around the sleeping cowboys wrapped in blankets, lying by the embers of last night's campfire. He doesn't need a lantern. His 'chuck wagon' is so familiar to him, he could cook blindfolded.

Cookie pulls out the drawer where he keeps the coffee. The cowboys like their coffee thick and strong. 'Boil the coffee till a horseshoe floats in it!' That's what they always say. Cookie is the most important person on the trail ride. He knows good food and strong coffee keep the cowboys happy.

The chuck wagon was invented by Texas rancher Charles Goodnight in 1866. He needed a sturdy movable kitchen which would serve trail crews for the long cattle drive. Goodnight took a canvas-topped army wagon and hung a large water barrel on the side, holding enough water for two days. The 'chuck box' was a set of drawers and cubbyholes at the back of the wagon, as neat and well-organized as the food compartments on a modern airplane. The hinged lid of the box folded down to make a work table. The chuck box held flour, sugar, coffee and spices, also needle and thread, razors and medicines. Cookie was the trail doctor and barber, and he sewed on buttons as well. No wonder he was sometimes called 'Old Lady'!

They may have teased him, but the cowboys respected Cookie. They knew better than to ride their horses through the kitchen area, or to eat at his work table. It was also polite to ride downwind of the chuck wagon, so dust didn't blow in the food.

For his hungry cowboys, Cookie usually prepared stew with beans, maybe rice as well, and a little salt pork for flavor. This was cooked in a pot hanging over the campfire made of 'prairie coal' - dried cow or buffalo dung. He might also make sour dough biscuits, baked in a special 'dutch oven', a pot which was placed right in the glowing coals.

If someone shot a prairie chicken or jackrabbit then there was meat to break the monotony of beans and bacon. Steers were worth a lot once they reached the market, so the cowboys enjoyed beef when a calf broke a leg and had to be shot.

Cookie had to make do with whatever supplies he could pack in a chuck wagon, plus any berries or fruit found on the way. He could even make a 'mock apple pie' using crackers instead of apples! If they camped near a town, he might buy cans of fruit or more flour and coffee. The used cans weren't thrown away - they made good measuring cups.

Pretend you are out on the trail and make a meal with whatever ingredients you have in your house! Get permission to use the kitchen and ask for help in cooking. Then look in the refrigerator and pantry to see what things might go together to make a stew. Here's one I made from items in my own kitchen:

HOME TRAIL STEW

(You will need: a knife and cutting board, a carrot peeler, measuring cups and spoons, a large pot and a large spoon for stirring)

Ingredients: 1 carrot, peeled and sliced into rings

1 stalk of celery, washed and chopped

1 can chopped tomatoes

4 cups (1 liter) chicken broth - made with boiling water and a chicken stock cube

1 can red kidney beans in chili sauce

1 teaspoon dried onion flakes

1 teaspoon dried parsley

1/2 teaspoon salt

1/8 teaspoon ground black pepper

2 or 3 handfuls of sliced spicy sausage

(You may leave the meat out)

A few handfuls of leftover cooked rice

Stir all ingredients together in the pot. Bring to a boil over a high heat. Then reduce heat and cover the pan. Simmer on low for 30-40 minutes, stirring every so often. This will make 3-4 servings.

Your stew may be completely different from this. I wonder what interesting ingredients you will find?

The diet of the early pioneers was not the same as the cowboy on the trail. The mainstay of their meals was corn. That was the first crop they planted when they arrived in the wilderness, as they could use it to feed their animals and themselves.

Do you ever say 'Not this again!' when you see what's on the dinner table? Pioneer children would have been saying that at every meal - corn fritters, johnnycakes (cornmeal pancakes), sandwiches made from corn bread with molasses for lunch! It's hard for us to imagine eating the same thing all the time, but that was just part of making a home in the wilderness. Later they would grow other crops such as beans, onion and squash. They also ate whatever wild game they could find. Deer were plentiful, and they could hunt bear, wild boar and turkey.

This was before electricity or refrigerators. How could they keep the huge cuts of meat from a deer or wild boar fresh? They couldn't. All the meat had to be smoked in order to preserve it, and for that they needed a special hut called the smokehouse. The meat was salted first to remove all moisture, and then hung over a low smoky fire for several weeks until fully cured. Nothing was wasted: the run-off from the hardwood fire was a strong liquid called lye, which they used to make soap.

As followers of Jesus, God provides 'food' for our souls. This soul food is found in the Bible, which is God's message to us. He wants us to learn to read his book, so we can understand who he is and what he has in mind for us. If we never read the Bible, we may be going hungry! Start by reading the book of Mark in the New Testament section. That will tell you lots of exciting things that Jesus did during his life on earth. Ask someone who has been a Christian for a while to help you understand God's special book.

In the Wild West today, some people still hunt for wild game. They do it for sport, yet none of the meat is wasted. If the hunter does not use it, then he gives it to charities or people who need it. While hunting deer may sound cruel, it is one way to manage the population. In many parts of the West there are too many deer, and hunting helps keep the numbers under control. This means there will be enough food to go around in the winter. Otherwise, many deer will starve.

Meat from a deer is called 'venison'. It is a very lean meat, so often it is mixed with more fatty meat like pork to improve the flavor, and made into sausage. 'Field dressing' a deer is important, to keep it from having a gamey taste. As soon as the deer is dead, you slit the animal from the chin all the way down, and remove its insides. Quickly hang it up in a tree, so that the blood can drain out. Next, use several buckets of water to wash out the insides and let it dry. Then skin it, leaving the bare carcass hanging outside overnight if the weather is cool enough.

Once the deer has been butchered, the yield is about forty pounds (eighteen kilograms) of meat from one deer. If you are a city dweller this all may sound very yucky! Yet this is one way that food is obtained in the West today.

What are your favorite foods? I am very fond of popcorn, Mexican food, and chocolate. I suppose we could get all of our nutrients simply by swallowing a pill, but wouldn't that be boring! God offers us spiritual food that is delicious and totally satisfying to our inner, spiritual selves.

Reading God's book is just one way to get the nourishment that helps you grow. Another way is by talking to God in prayer. You don't have to use a special way of speaking when you talk to God - he just wants you to be yourself. He knows all about you, but he wants you to tell him about anything that is bothering you or about something that makes you happy. Take time to talk to God every day, and don't forget to thank him for being so awesome!

Let the words of Christ, in all their richness, live in your hearts and make you wise... Sing psalms and hymns and spiritual songs to God with thankful hearts. (Colossians 3:16)

Remember the Alamo!

Enrique Esparza was playing in the plaza outside the old Alamo mission in San Antonio with his brothers and sister. Their family were 'Tejanos', Mexicans who lived in the Mexican territory of Texas. There had been some trouble between the government of Mexico and the Texan settlers, but Enrique wasn't thinking about that. He was simply enjoying playing.

The children heard some noise - it sounded like a band. Was there a festival they didn't know about? Suddenly the plaza was full of soldiers in bright red and blue uniforms with swords at their belts. Enrique's eye was caught by a tall mounted soldier wearing red braid. It was the Mexican General Santa Anna himself! The Esparza family had intended to escape before the Mexican army arrived, but they were too late. They were forced to take shelter in the Alamo mission, where a group of Texans and their friends had holed up, ready to defend themselves.

In 1821 the Mexican government had begun offering cheap land to anyone from the US who wanted to settle in Texas, and people poured in from as far away as Europe. By 1830, about 20,000 settlers had come and the government began to be worried that there were too many. They tried to stop more from coming.

When the Texans protested, the President-General, Santa Anna, sent his troops under General Cos to San Antonio, which was the capital of Texas at that time. The Texans gave Cos a humiliating defeat. Santa Anna was furious. He thought of himself as 'the Napoleon of the West'. Who did these ignorant farmers and hunters imagine they were, to defeat his army? He gathered his soldiers together and marched north from Mexico. He would not rest until the Texans were destroyed.

Meanwhile, a small group of Texan soldiers plus a few women and children had gathered inside the Alamo. It was a huge compound, which would have needed a thousand soldiers to defend properly. The Texan leader Colonel William Travis had been writing letters pleading for help. 'To the People of Texas and all Americans in the world,' Travis wrote, 'I shall never surrender or retreat... Victory or Death!'

Travis urgently needed more men and supplies. But only a handful of people responded. There were less than 200 soldiers at the Alamo when Santa Anna's army arrived. The Texans were outnumbered twenty to one.

Enrique and his family crowded together in the dark corner of a shuttered room inside the Alamo compound. They felt scared and helpless. They must have heard the men shouting in the courtyard outside, one voice rising above the rest. That was tall Jim Bowie, yelling for the soldiers to build platforms from which they could shoot at the enemy.

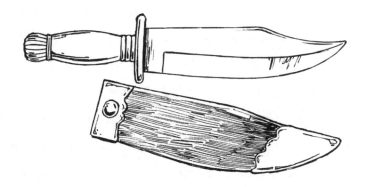

Bowie had a special large hunting knife which he would use on a wounded bear if he didn't have time to reload his weapon. He had also used it to kill men in fights. This weapon which looked like a butcher knife became famous, and from then on that sort of knife was called a Bowie knife.

The Texans got their ammunition ready: they broke up old horseshoes to use in the cannon, and prepared bullets, gunpowder and ramrods for loading their flintlock rifles. When they ran out of bullets, they would have to use knives or their fists.

The Mexican army carried heavy English 'Brown Bess' muskets, which had a deadly bayonet attached to the end. The Texans' hunting rifles could shoot much further with accuracy but took three times as long to load. However, the Mexican soldiers had not been trained to use their muskets. Some of them might end up shooting each other.

Do you have your weapons ready? Are you trained to use them? I don't mean guns and swords, but your faith weapons. The Bible says that as followers of Jesus, we have an enemy. He is sometimes called Satan, or the Devil. He tries very hard to make sure we are not happy as Christians. He'll even try to stop you believing in God in the first place. But Jesus has already defeated this enemy. When Jesus died on the cross and then came back to life after three days, that was a tremendous show of God's power over Satan. In spite of that, the enemy still has a great deal of influence in this world.

What weapons do Christians have? Trusting in Jesus to save us, obeying him, living by faith, reading the Bible, talking to God in prayer - these are some of the things we need in order to be strong in our friendship with Jesus.

The Texans were as ready as they could be, with their few numbers and limited ammunition. Suddenly Enrique heard a tremendous *boom*. It was the noise of the Texan's giant cannon, letting Santa Anna know they had no intention of surrendering.

The Mexican General responded by bombarding the fortress with cannon and musket fire. Day and night for twelve days the noise raged. The air was thick with the sharp smell of exploding gunpowder. During these terrible days, the legendary Davy

Crockett played his fiddle to try and cheer up the men - when he wasn't shooting at the Mexicans with his favorite long rifle, 'Old Betsy'. He had arrived a couple of weeks before with some other men from Tennessee, saying, "We heard you were having trouble with the likes of old Santy Anny and ... we like a good fight!'

Up until the end of the siege, the Texans had not lost a single man, though Bowie was very ill. On the thirteenth day, everything went quiet. Santa Anna was going to let the Texans have a rest, then mount a surprise attack while they were sleeping.

During these hours of peace before the final storm, Colonel Travis reportedly called his men together and arranged them in a single line in the courtyard. Jim Bowie was carried outside on his camp bed to join them. Travis drew his sword and traced a line in the dirt between him and his men. By then it was clear that help was not going to come.

'Within a very few days,' Travis said, 'perhaps a very few hours - we must all be in eternity.' But he gave the men a choice. They could either die like cowards or bravely, fighting to the very end. Those who were willing to fight on, should step over the line. According to the story, all but one did. Bowie even asked for his bed to be carried across the line.

Travis was one of the first to die when Santa Anna's troops stormed the Alamo before dawn the next morning. He was only 26 years old.

Once the Mexican army broke through the Alamo defense, it was all over quickly. None of the Texan soldiers were spared. The only people allowed to live were a handful of women, children and slaves. Enrique would remember the Alamo tragedy for the rest of his life. His only consolation was that his father was granted a proper burial by Santa Anna, because his father's brother had fought earlier in the Mexican army. The rest of the Texan bodies were stacked in heaps, doused with fuel and burned. It was a horrible end to what began as a noble cause.

And yet, it was not the end. 'Remember the Alamo!' became the battle cry for the remaining residents of Texas. Their anger over the slaughter of their comrades fueled the battle between General Sam Houston's troops and Santa Anna six weeks later. In a surprise attack near Galveston, the Texan army killed 600 Mexican soldiers in less than half an hour, and took the rest prisoner. Texas was free. It became an independent republic and later joined the Union as the 28th state.

The Alamo battle was just one of many, large and small, which were fought all over the West in the nineteenth century. Although it ended in defeat, it sparked a major victory and caught the imagination of many. We 'remember the Alamo' even today for the courage with which the Texans took a stand and faced the enemy.

Maybe you will someday be in a situation where, like the Alamo defenders, you have to stand firm for what you believe. If someone is making jokes or ugly remarks about Christians, do you have the courage to speak up? When your friends want to do something you know is wrong, do you refuse? Do you admit to being a follower of Jesus, even if others around you are not? Jesus said he would send his Spirit to be with his followers and help them.

If you belong to Jesus, then his Spirit is always with you. You can ask him to help you to be bold for his sake, when you need to be.

'Be strong with the Lord's mighty power. Put on all of God's armor so that you will be able to stand firm against all strategies and tricks of the Devil.' (Ephesians 6:10)

From Horses to Helicopters

The calves are bawling like babies and kicking up plenty of dust, as they charge around frantically on one side of the large corral. There's a sizzling noise as the branding iron connects with cowhide, and the smell of burning hair hits your nostrils. You're the wrangler - it's your job to rope the next calf to be branded. You spin your lasso above your head - you want to time your throw exactly, keeping an eye on the calf's legs and the way your horse is moving - now! You toss the loop out and it sails down to lie against the calf's hind legs. The calf steps into it.

There! You tighten the rope and your horse pulls back in the same instant, holding the rope taut. Your trusty mount has done this many times before and knows exactly what you expect of him. Just then the phone in your pocket rings. You ignore it - it's probably your mother, wondering when you'll be home. It won't be anytime soon. There's a juddering roar overhead as the helicopter heads out to another pasture, to herd the next batch of cows towards the corral. Even though it takes a team of cowboys only about a minute to brand, de-horn and vaccinate a calf, as well as clip a tag onto its ear, there are still a few hundred left to 'work'.

You would see this combination of the old and the new on most working ranches today. Helicopters or all-terrain vehicles are cheaper and faster than horses for rounding up cattle. Frightened by the noise, the calves will stay together and run in the direction they are herded. Some ranches never use horses at all - the animals are herded through a series of steel pens and then each guided one by one into a hydraulically controlled 'squeeze chute', which holds the calf still for the couple of minutes needed to treat it.

Today most calves wear plastic ear tags so they can be identified at a distance. However, they also need a permanent mark, as cattle rustling costs ranchers millions of dollars each year. Cattle are often branded in the traditional way, although usually with an electric branding iron. Some ranches use electronic tags or freeze branding. Whatever method is used, the main thing is that the animals are protected from being stolen.

Horses rather than trucks may still be used to herd the cattle into the pens and to work them once they are there, or to round up a cow that's too wild. Also, there are places such as a tight ravine where a wheeled vehicle can't go. Then the rancher goes in on horseback to slowly coax a stray calf back to the corral.

Even on the most modern ranches, the personal touch of the cowboy is needed. For example, when the cows are about to give birth, the ranch hands check on them once or twice a day to make sure there are no problems. Once the babies are born, the cowboys watch closely to see which calves belong to which mothers. How do they know? The animals tell them! Each newborn calf knows the scent and sound of its own mother, and the mother knows the calf. In a whole pasture full of milling, mooing cattle, they can find each other without any problem. When the new calf wants to feed, it butts its nose against the full udder of the mother. This makes the milk drop down into the canal of the teat, so the calf can get to it.

How are these baby calves so smart? Do you think things like that just happen by chance? They don't. God has designed our world so wonderfully well, that every detail is in place. We may say the animals use 'instinct' because they know without anyone telling them - yet God has planned it that way.

Some of the old-time cowboy skills such as 'cutting out' a calf from the herd, are still practiced today at special events called rodeos. The cutting horses are often Quarter Horses, originally bred to race the quarter mile. Their compact bodies help them perform the quick, tricky moves needed in working cattle, and they have an innate 'cow sense'. This was the horse used most often by the cowboy on the range.

Wild mustangs also have good 'cow sense'. Growing up on the open range, they are tough, healthy horses which tend to be calm and easy-going once they have been trained. Today, the US Bureau of Land Management offers mustangs for adoption to good homes. Many people who work with wild horses don't believe in 'breaking' a horse - they use the term 'gentling' instead. The goal is for the horse to become the cowboy's partner. If it likes its owner, it will be obedient.

A first-class cutting horse knows how to follow a calf with hardly any direction from the reins. When the calf swerves and darts off in another direction, the horse can stop short from a full gallop and spring away after it.

Other rodeo events include bronco 'busting', in which the cowboy tries to ride an untamed horse without getting thrown off. In steer 'wrestling' the cowboy grabs a young bull by its horns and quickly twists it to the ground.

At the height of the Wild West, about 40,000 cowboys in the US worked with cattle. Today the numbers are much fewer. Yet those who still ride the range speak of the freedom of being out in the open country, the special relationship with their horse, the adventure of each new day. 'Cowboying' as it is called, is a good way to learn patience and the value of hard work.

Based on the movies, you may think of cowboys as rowdy wild men, ready to shoot up the town. In fact, the modern ranch worker often has a faith in God. He or she is like a shepherd, taking care of what God has provided in his creation.

He is often what we call a 'good Samaritan', as well. This comes from a story Jesus told about a man from the country of Samaria who helped someone he saw lying injured in the road. At the end of this story Jesus asked his listeners, 'Who is your neighbor?' The cowboy might reply, 'Whoever needs my help.' If a rancher sees a broken fence with someone else's cows wandering in the road, he will drive the cattle back into the pasture and repair the fence himself.

Who is *your* neighbor? Think about that for a moment. It may not mean the person who lives next door to you. Is there someone you know who could use your help?

In the time of the Wild West, it was said there was 'no law west of the Missouri River and no God west of Fort Smith' in Arkansas. That was not true, as God is everywhere, even in dark places. He was worshipped quietly by families living in pioneer homes, who had only an occasional visit from a traveling preacher. As towns grew up, churches were built where people could come together and learn about God and praise him.

What about the West today? Of course there are thousands of churches of every description, but something new is happening.

You can go to a church where everybody is wearing western clothing. It might meet in a school or even outdoors under a tree.

The music may sound familiar because the tunes are from the top 40 country songs, but the words are rewritten to honor God.

There are hundreds of 'cowboy churches' in the West today. They often serve barbecue at church dinners, and use rodeo events as a means of reaching out with the Good News about Jesus. New Christians who want to be baptized may be dunked in a watering trough! These are churches where anyone who loves horses and the cowboy way of life, can feel comfortable. They know the church accepts them the way they are and that God does too.

Your church may be very different from a cowboy church, but I do hope you attend one. There are no perfect churches, just as there are no perfect people. But we need each other. We need to be in a place where we can hear the Bible and worship God with other Christians. God places us in families and communities and groups of Christians. That's how he wants us to grow!

One part of growing as a Christian is telling others about what Jesus means to you. Getting to know Jesus is the most exciting thing that can happen to a person. Wouldn't you want to pass that on to your family and friends? Being part of a church can help you be bold in speaking up.

The Wild West is no longer so wild, and most of the country has been settled. Yet the West still exists, even if partly in our imagination. There are many places today where we can get a glimpse of what it might have been like to live in the time when the harsh land was untamed and the cowboy was king.

Did you ever think that you can be like a Wild West traveler? When you are on a journey of faith, it can be as exciting and full of adventure as anything the pioneers or cowboys experienced. It's all about understanding that God loves you very much, and learning to live as a follower of Jesus. Perhaps like the people of the West, you will find that life isn't always easy. Yet God has many surprising and wonderful things in store for you. You can step out with confidence day by day, in the amazing quest of knowing him!

No eye has seen, no ear has heard, and no mind has imagined what God has prepared for those who love him. (1 Corinthians 2:9)

WILD WEST QUIZ

1. What was the word for an unbranded calf over six months old?

2. Why is it not a good idea to fire a gun during a cattle drive?

3. Who is the desert garbage collector?

4. How does the cottonmouth snake get its name?

5. How is Jesus like a lifeguard?

6. What is strange about a roadrunner's tracks?

7. Why is learning to wait important for a Christian?

8. What are clones?

9. What are the ingredients of pemmican sausage?

10. What was the buffalo hunter's prize?

11. What kind of litter was found on the Oregon Trail?

12. Why were the pioneer family walking instead of riding?

13. Where is Jesus making a new home for us?

14. How was Wyatt Earp able to draw his gun easily?

15. Which two guns were called 'the gun that won the West'?

16. What is the best way to bring peace into a conflict?

17. What was stagecoach driver Charley Parkhurst's secret?

18. What were the first pioneer homes on the prairie?

19. What did children have to eat when they had the measles?

20. What was 'prairie coal'?

21. What was the main food for the early pioneers?

22. What are two ways to get nourishment to grow as Christians?

23. How did the Alamo soldiers make cannon balls?

24. What are some of the Christians' weapons?

25. What is the cheapest way of rounding up cattle today?

26. How do newborn calves in a herd find their mothers?

27. What is the most exciting thing that can happen to a person?

ANSWERS TO WILD WEST QUIZ

1. A maverick.

2. The cattle might stampede.

3. The vulture.

4. Its mouth looks like it is filled with cotton.

5. He will save us when we call for help.

6. Two toes point forwards and two point backwards.

7. It is one way that we show God we are trusting him.

8. Exact copies of a plant or animal.

9. Dried buffalo meat, berries and melted buffalo fat.

10. The raw buffalo liver eaten straight from the dead animal.

11. Pianos and pieces of furniture.

12. Horses were expensive. There was no room in the wagon.

13. In Heaven.

14. His coat pocket was lined with canvas and wax.

15. The Winchester '73 and the Colt six-shooter.

16. Forgiveness.

17. Charley was a woman.

18. Underground dug-outs or houses made from sod bricks.

19. Well-roasted mouse.

20. Dried buffalo or cow dung.

21. Corn.

22. Reading the Bible and talking to God.

23. They broke up old horseshoes.

24. Trusting Jesus to save us, obeying him, living by faith, reading the Bible, talking to God.

25. With a helicopter or all-terrain vehicle.

26. They recognise their mother's scent and sound.

27. Getting to know Jesus.

ABOUT THE AUTHOR

Donna Vann always wanted to be a writer, because books meant so much to her when she was younger. She kept notebooks of her stories but did not begin writing books until she had three children of her own. Donna grew up in Texas. She and her husband work with an international Christian charity called Agapé Europe, and have lived in the UK for many years. She may be contacted via her website, www.donnavann.com

Other books by Donna Vann:

Corin's Quest

ISBN: 978-1-85792-218-9

King Arthur's Ransom

ISBN: 978-1-85792-849-5

Which Way you gonna' Jump?

ISBN: 978-1-85792-368-1

The Adventures Series
An ideal series to collect

Have you ever wanted to visit the rainforest? Have you ever longed to sail down the Amazon river? Would you just love to go on Safari in Africa? Well these books can help you imagine that you are actually there.

Pioneer missionaries retell their amazing adventures and encounters with animals and nature. In the Amazon you will discover tree frogs, piranha fish and electric eels. In the Rainforest you will be amazed at the armadillo and the toucan. In the blistering heat of the African Savannah you will come across lions and elephants and hyenas. And you will discover how God is at work in these amazing environments.

Rainforest Adventures by Horace Banner
ISBN 978-1-85792-627-9

African Adventures by Dick Anderson
ISBN 978-1-85792-807-5

Amazon Adventures by Horace Banner
ISBN 978-1-85792-440-4

Cambodian Adventures by Donna Vann
ISBN 978-1-84550-474-8

Great Barrier Reef Adventures by Jim Cromarty
ISBN 978-1-84550-068-9

Himalayan Adventures by Penny Reeve
ISBN 978-1-84550-080-1

Kiwi Adventures by Bartha Hill
ISBN 978-1-84550-282-9

New York City Adventures by Donna Vann
ISBN 978-1-84550-546-2

Outback Adventures by Jim Cromarty
ISBN 978-1-85792-974-4

Pacific Adventures by Jim Cromarty
ISBN 978-1-84550-475-5

Rainforest Adventures by Horace Banner
ISBN 978-1-85792-627-9

Rocky Mountain Adventures by Betty Swinford
ISBN 978-1-85792-962-1

Scottish Highland Adventures by Catherine Mackenzie
ISBN 978-1-84550-281-2

Wild West Adventures by Donna Vann
ISBN 978-1-84550-065-8

CHRISTIAN FOCUS PUBLICATIONS

Christian Focus   **Christian Heritage**   **CF4K**   **Mentor**

Christian Focus Publications publishes books for adults and children under its four main imprints: Christian Focus, Christian Heritage, CF4K and Mentor. Our books reflect that God's word is reliable and Jesus is the way to know him, and live for ever with him.

Our children's publication list includes a Sunday school curriculum that covers pre-school to early teens; puzzle and activity books. We also publish personal and family devotional titles, biographies and inspirational stories that children will love.

If you are looking for quality Bible teaching for children then we have an excellent range of Bible story and age specific theological books.

From pre-school to teenage fiction, we have it covered!

Find us at our web page:
www.christianfocus.com

CF4 •K
Because you're never too young to know Jesus